walk with me.
a great-grandmother's story

a guided journal of memories
for my great-grandchild

Other Books In The "Walk With Me" Series:

A Great-Grandfather's Story
A Grandmother's Story
A Grandfather's Story
A Mother's Story
A Father's Story
A Stepmother's Story
A Stepfather's Story
A Sister's Story

wandering tortoise

Copyright 2020 Patricia N. Hicks. All rights reserved.

No part of this publication may be reproduced, distributed or transmitted
in any form or by any means, including photocopying, recording,
or other electronic or mechanical methods, without prior
written permission of the author, except as permitted by US copyright law.

ISBN: 979-8689210742

Introduction

This guided journal is a fantastic way to create a
one-of-a-kind keepsake for your great-grandchild!

Includes 134 thought-provoking writing prompts
written from the perspective of your great-grandchild.
Write as though you are speaking directly to them.

You can choose to complete one page a day or several at once.
Pages can be completed in any order you desire.

Also includes:
A Six-Generation Family Tree
Two Recipe Pages
Two Dot Grid Pages For Drawing Diagrams
(floor plans, property boundaries, room layout, etc)

There are plenty of places for writing, but there are also
empty pages at the beginning and end of each section that can be
filled with photographs, clippings, and anything else you wish
to include to help bring your stories to life.

Family

Childhood

Teenage Years

Adulthood

Love & Marriage

Parenting

More About You

Looking Back

Looking Forward

Your Full Name

Your Date of Birth

Your Place of Birth

the date you began this journal

the person you are completing this journal for

Family

Our

Your Paternal Grandfather
_____
B: _____ D: _____

M: _____

Your Paternal Grandmother
_____
B: _____ D: _____

Your Father
_____
B: _____ D: _____

M: _____

Your Maternal Grandfather
_____
B: _____ D: _____

M: _____

Your Maternal Grandmother
_____
B: _____ D: _____

Your Mother
_____
B: _____ D: _____

B = Born
M = Married
D = Died

Family Tree

You

B: _____

My Great-Grandfather

B: _____ D: _____

M: _____

My Grandparent (your child)

B: _____ D: _____

My Grandparent

B: _____ D: _____

M: _____

My Parent (your grandchild)

B: _____ D: _____

My Parent

B: _____ D: _____

M: _____

Me (your great-grandchild)

Where did your name come from?
Does it have special meaning?
Were you named after a family member?

Did you have a nickname that everyone called you? How did you get that nickname? What do family members call you now?

Describe your mother.
When you think of her, which of her characteristics stand out the most?

*What is your favorite memory
of your mother?*

*Describe your father.
Which of his characteristics stand out
the most in your mind?*

What is your favorite memory of your father?

*Do you feel you more closely resemble your mother or your father?
In what way?*

Were you able to see your grandparents often when you were young? Where did they live? What were they like?

*Did your grandparents ever tell stories about their past?
What did you learn about them?*

*Did you know your great-grandparents?
Describe them.*

Do you have any brothers or sisters? What was your relationship like when you were younger? What is it like now?

Were you the oldest child, middle child, youngest child or the only child? What advantages or disadvantages do you feel this gave you?

How did your family spend quality time together?

What do you feel was the most important lesson your parents taught you?

Knowing what you know now, is there anything you wish your parents had taught you but didn't?

What expectations or aspirations did your family have for your future?

Is there anything you wish you had asked your parents or grandparents? What is it and why? Is there anything you wish they had asked you?

Childhood

What is your earliest memory?

Describe your childhood home.
If you had more than one, describe your favorite.

Draw a layout of your childhood home or yard.

Did you grow up in a two-parent household, a single-parent home or with someone else? How do you feel this has impacted your life?

What occupations did your parents or guardians have? Did you see them often or were they frequently away for work?

Describe what a typical day was like in your home.

As a child, what did you want to be when you grew up?
Did anything influence this decision?

What types of chores were you expected to do?
Was there a chore that you especially
liked or disliked?

Did you get an allowance?
How much was it?
What did you typically spend it on?

Do you have a favorite holiday tradition from your childhood? What is it, and why is it your favorite?

What was your favorite childhood toy, game, or activity?

Did you have any childhood illnesses or diseases or any notable medical emergencies?

Is there a frightening memory from your childhood that you still remember vividly today?

Did you have a favorite bedtime story when you were a child? Did you read this same story to your own children at bedtime?

Did you have an idol or hero as a child? Why was this particular person your favorite?

What was your favorite meal growing up?
Who made it?
Do you still enjoy it today?

If you know the recipe, please share it.

Recipe: _____

# of Servings: _____

Ingredients:

Instructions:

Who or what do you remember most fondly from your childhood?

Teenage Years

What school did you attend during your teenage years? Did you enjoy school? Would you have preferred a different school?

What was your school dress code? Describe what you would typically wear to school.

Did you participate in school sports, clubs or other school activities?

Describe your typical day at school.

What was your favorite school subject or your favorite teacher? Why?

What class did you find the easiest? What class was the most challenging for you?

Did you participate in a youth group or youth organization? How has this experience influenced your adult life?

*What trends or fads were popular
when you were young?
Did you participate in those fads?*

What did you and your friends like to do for fun? Did you have a favorite hangout?

*What types of music did you like back then?
Who are some of your favorite musicians
or bands from your teenage years?*

Did you have a best friend or group of friends as a teenager? What things would you do together?

How old were you when you started dating?
Where did you typically go on dates?

Did you have a curfew? What time was it? What would happen if you missed curfew?

Did you have a job when you were a teenager?
What was it? How much were you paid?
What responsibilities did you have?

At any time during your youth, did you save your money for something special? What was it? How did you earn the money for it?

Did you ever get into trouble as a teenager? What kinds of consequences would you face?

When you were a teenager, did you have any idea what path you wanted to take after high school? What influenced your decision?

Adulthood

Did you receive any education or training beyond high school? What was it? Did you earn any degrees or certifications?

What jobs have you had in your adult life?

What was your favorite job?
How much did the job pay?
Why was it your favorite?

Can you drive a car?
Who taught you to drive?

*When did you get your first car?
How did the ability to drive
change your lifestyle?*

Did you serve in the military? If so, in what branch of service? For how long? What was your rank? Where were you stationed?

What is your most memorable moment from your time in the military?

Describe your first house or apartment. What did you do to make it a home?

Draw a layout of your first home.

What organizations or groups have you belonged to as an adult? How did you become involved in them?

When did you begin to feel you were really an adult and not just playing the part?

Love & Marriage

*How many serious personal relationships have you been in?
What did you learn from them?*

Tell me about the hardest breakup you've experienced. How did you heal from it?

What is the most difficult relationship challenge you have had to face? Were you able to overcome it? How?

*How did you meet my great-grandfather?
How old were the two of you?*

Describe your first date with my great-grandfather. What did you find attractive about him?

Was my great-grandfather able to meet your parents? What was their impression of him?

Did you get married? What made you feel sure you chose the right person to be your life partner?

Describe your wedding ceremony.
Who was there to celebrate with you?

*Did you have a honeymoon?
If so, where did you go? What is a fun
memory about your honeymoon?*

Have you been married more than once?
How do you feel those marriages
differed from each other?

What advice about relationships, love and marriage can you share with me?

Parenting

How did you feel when you realized you were going to be a mother? Who was the first person you told?

Were you given any parenting advice?
What was the advice?
Who gave you the advice?

How many children have you had?
Tell me about them. Describe their differences.

How did you choose names for your child / children? Are they named after special people in your life?

*Tell me about the day
my grandmother / grandfather was born.*

What is your favorite memory of my grandmother/ grandfather from their youth?

How did you feel when your children started school? Were you excited for them? Nervous? Scared?

Do you feel you were a strict parent or a lenient parent? Why do you feel that way?

*Is your parenting style similar to
the way you were raised or is it different?
Is that by choice or circumstance?*

What do you feel was the most difficult part of raising a child?

What was your scariest moment as a parent?

Describe a rewarding moment in your life as a parent.

If you could turn back time, would you choose to raise your family differently? What would you change?

*Is there a favorite family recipe you make?
Tell its history or share a story about it.*

Share your family's favorite recipe.

Recipe: _____

# of Servings: _____

Ingredients:

Instructions:

What advice did you give your children (or grandchildren) about parenting?

How did you feel when you found out you were going to be a great-grandmother?

What is your favorite thing about being a grandmother and great-grandmother?

How do you feel when you look at your family and see three generations of your descendants?

More About You

*How would you describe yourself?
Creative? Funny? Logical?
Generous? Impulsive? Compassionate?*

Is there anything about yourself that you would change if you could? What is it and why?

What hobbies do you have? Is there a special reason you began these hobbies?

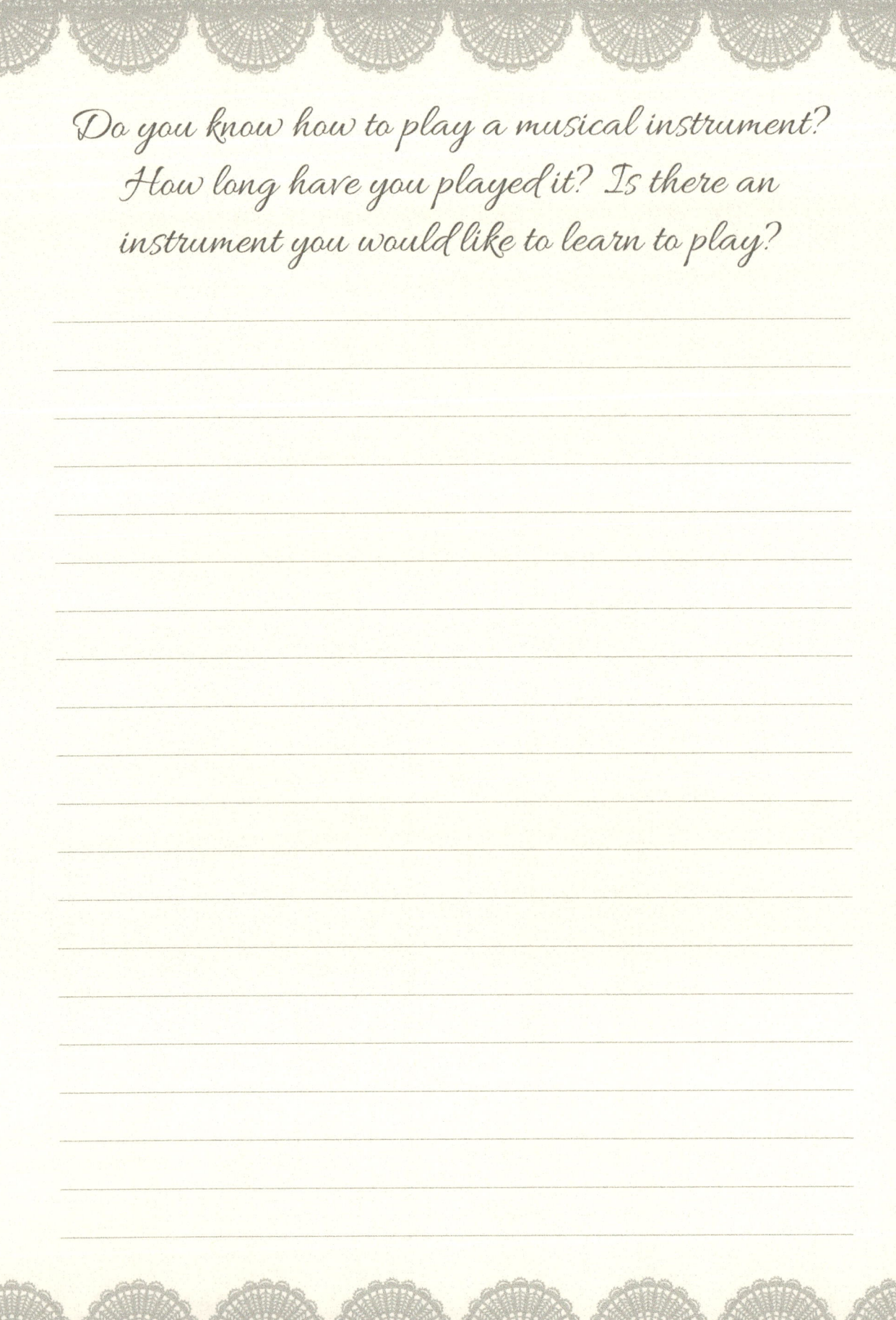

Do you know how to play a musical instrument? How long have you played it? Is there an instrument you would like to learn to play?

Have you received any special awards or recognitions in your life? What were they, and when did you receive them?

*Do you practice a religion?
If so, is it the same religion as
your parents and grandparents?*

How do you feel religion has influenced your life?

*What is your favorite holiday?
What do you love about it?*

Who is your best friend?
How long have you known them?
What draws you to them?

What are your "good habits"?
Do you have any "bad habits"?

Do you have a special or unusual talent?

Favorites

Food: _____

Cuisine: _____

Dessert: _____

Drink: _____

Candy: _____

Game or Sport: _____

Athlete: _____

Book: _____

Author: _____

Television Show: _____

Movie: _____

Movie Genre: _____

Actor or Actress: _____

Composer: _____

Song: _____

Singer: _____

Music Genre: _____

Animal: _____

Vacation Destination: _____

Thing You Can't Live Without: _____

Favorites

Pastime: _____

Modern Convenience: _____

Place to Shop: _____

Gadget or Tool: _____

Flower: _____

Person in History: _____

House Style: _____

Color: _____

Artist: _____

Article of Clothing: _____

Motivational Speaker: _____

Type of Weather: _____

Way to Relax: _____

Warm Weather Activity: _____

Cold Weather Activity: _____

Season: _____

Holiday: _____

Car: _____

Thing to Collect: _____

Quote or Verse: _____

Looking Back

What has been your favorite age or stage in life so far?

What is the first theatrical play you remember seeing on stage? Did you enjoy it?

What is the first movie
you remember seeing in a theater?
How have movie theaters changed since then?

How many pets have you had?
Describe your favorite pet.

What was your initial reaction to computers and the internet? Have your views changed? Do you use them for shopping, research or socializing?

What is the best advice you have received?
Who gave you that advice?

Tell about a compliment you have received that has had an impact on your life.

*Describe a difficult choice
that you have had to make in your life.
How did you reach your decision?*

Who is someone you would like to see again? What would you say or do when you saw them?

Have you traveled much?
What places have you been?
What was your favorite place to visit?

What is your favorite vacation memory, either from your childhood or from a trip taken more recently?

Regarding world events and politics, how do you feel the views of your parents and grandparents have influenced your own perspective?

Have your political views changed over time from social influences or life experiences? How? Were there any particular events that caused this change?

What social issues of today did you also see during your childhood? Do you feel things have improved?

What are the most significant differences you see between the world of your childhood and the world today?

What hardships have you experienced in your life? What challenges did you face? How did you overcome those challenges?

What is something in your life you feel you would do differently if given the chance? What impact do you feel this change would have on your life?

What do you wish you had done more of in your life? What do you wish you had spent less time doing?

Have there been any wars in your lifetime? Were you or someone you know personally involved? How do you feel that time period has impacted your life?

*Do you have any unfulfilled dreams?
Something you have always wanted
to do but haven't?*

What do you like the most about your generation?
What do you like the least?

You've experienced a lifetime of history.
Did any historical events surprise or scare you?
Did any make you hopeful for the future?

Do you have any disappointments or regrets? Tell me about them.

What do you miss most about the world you grew up in? What do you feel has changed for the better?

Looking Forward

What are you looking forward to the most at this stage in your life?

Describe what your perfect day would be like.

What goals or dreams are you working on right now?

What skills or special knowledge do you have that you would like to pass down to the next generation?

What are some new skills you would like to learn?

What do you want your family and friends to learn from your life?

What family traditions do you hope future generations will continue to carry on?

What are some of the important "life lessons" you have gathered along the way?

How do you want to be remembered by future generations?

What do you feel is the secret to a long and fulfilling life?